STARDUST'S SPACE

BEYOND THE UNIVERSE

RUBEENA KAUR

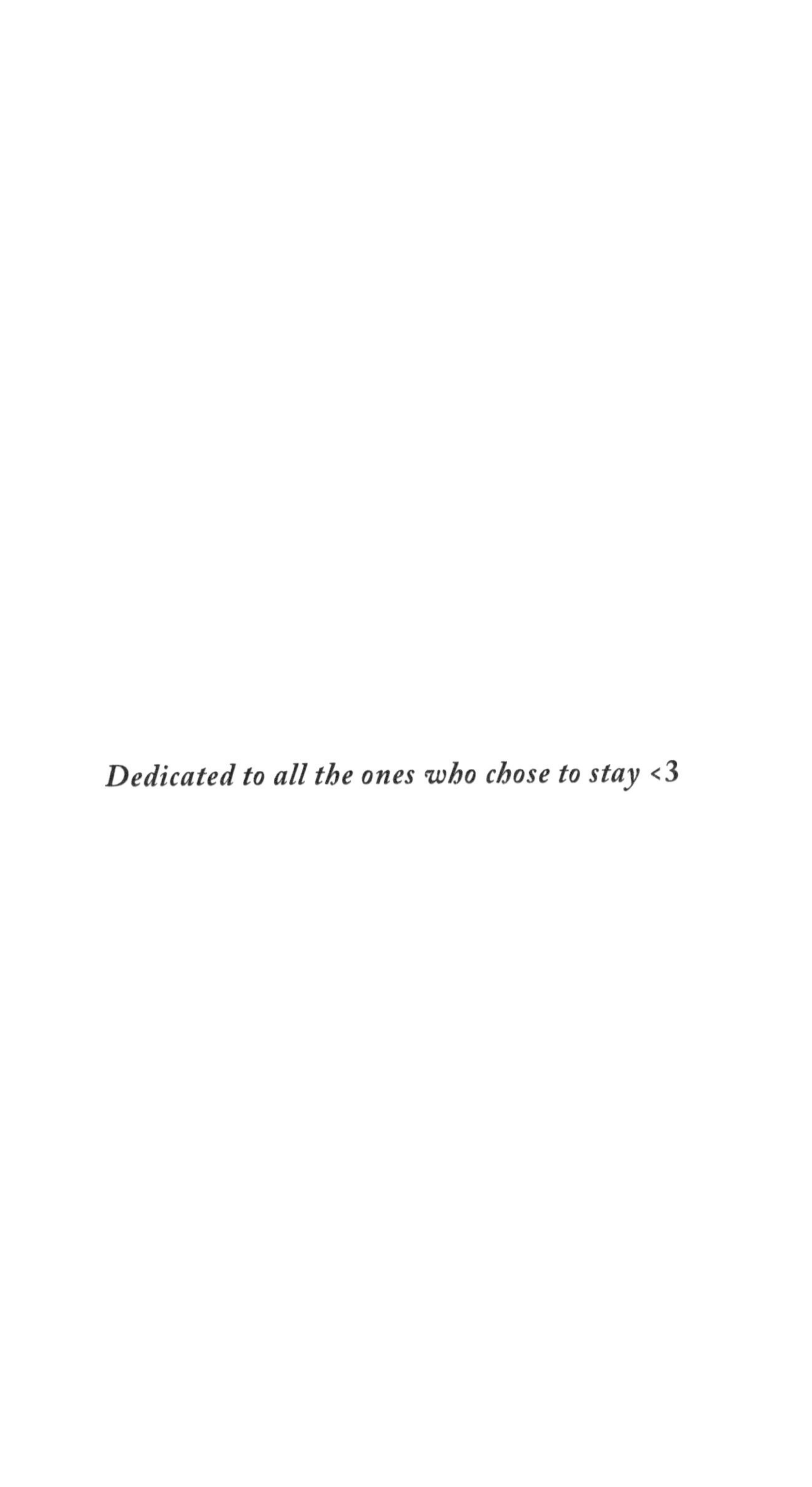

Dedicated to all the ones who chose to stay <3

Contents

Contents

ALWAYS & FOREVER

And that day the time would stop, waiting for me to capture that
perfect moment of happiness a million times. I promise to hold
onto that memory always & forever. Not letting it slip away even
if I get a thousand more. cause that one would love the calm and
rage in me, all at once. Floating gently around the core of my
'always & forever' for an eternity of love.

YIN

1. THE REAL LIES

Please just say; that's all not true,
that you still love me ; out of the blue.
that you still want me by you,
that everything you've lied about is true.

That I'm still the one that you want,
and leaving us is what our heads haunt.
even if you can't ; just take it back,
and tell me that you feel a piece of you lack.

Can't you just see right through?
and tell me that the lies are true?
that roses with thorns have grace,
and there's a lot of bad to embrace.

Even the slightest hug would suffice,
and tell me that I was never your sacrifice
you should try harder to hide the real lies,
to prevent us from bidding our goodbyes.

2. BROKEN SOUL ALIVE

Even when I'm broken; there's nothing to mend
that's just who I am and will be in the end.
being broken does not mean that I never pretend ,
well, I do sometimes and it's not like I want to amend.

What defines me are my flaws and scars,
i never said that there were no thorns in flowers.
yeah, there are times when i wonder 'why',
am I the only place where defaults lie?

Where ever I go; my scars will go along ,
i don't care if they make me weak or strong.
they are no one else's but my own ,
but again , i'm never going to stitch the torn.

All of my flaws; I'm going to consume,
and then, you'll see a damaged flower bloom.
you'll see a flawed creature arrive ,
and watch a broken soul alive.

3. CLUBS FROM SPADES

You're all that I see ahead,
after all the tears that we've shed.
if you ever hurt me , i wouldn't care,
cause I know intentionally; you wouldn't dare.

i hope that we're both together destined,
though our fate still remains undefined.
we should've known better than our fates,
maybe somehow loved the darkest shades.

'Forever' is an emotion and not just a word,
at least that's what my soul has heard.
to be with you is all that I have in my head ,
this is where by your love I'm led.

Your love is what transformed my heart,
like you're some sort of wild and calm art.
i hope a love like ours never fades,
and we never become the clubs from spades.

4. CAN'T STOP LOVING YOU

Roses with thorns; thorns like you,
but that's the only thing I can hold on to.
i'm breathing slow with tears in my eyes,
you're all I want ; everything else is my sacrifice.

just one more time , let me hold on tight,
even if there's nothing but darkness in sight.
sit with me under the stars,
while i'm bleeding out my scars.

I love you in every minute of the day,
heaven is where our destinies lay.
bringing us together by amending their mistake,
but why don't we know ; how long would it take?

Isn't it hard for you to say your goodbye?
you won't always be covered by the illusion and lies.
please soften your thorns before it's too late,
to change what they call a 'sealed fate'

5. WILL THE ROSES STILL BLOOM?

What if I'm lying on my death bed
half alive ; half dead?
will someone light up the flame ,
or will everything remain the same?
I wonder if I will be missed ?
and my thought be kissed?
or will the wind just take me away?
and my memories be left by the bay?
will you bother saying goodbye?
and sit by my grave when you'd want to cry?
will you still love me at the end?
or maybe for the same you'll just pretend?
Will the earth deep down accept me at all?
or is it just going to let my spirit fall?
are the trees going to stand tall?
and shed some flowers if I call?
Will I love my dark and hollow coffin?
and will death come for me very often?
and will the roses still bloom
when I'll be lying dead inside my tomb?

6. I TELL MY SMILE

I tell my smile every now and then
hide my pain till the end of the day
don't worry the tears will shed when
i will sit alone and let all of it go away

I tell my smile to make me feel alive
so that in this harsh world i can survive
I wait for the arrival of the dark and gloomy night
so that I wash it away when there's no one in sight

I tell my smile each and every minute
that to fake itself there is no limit
and that it turns the world blind
because my invisible scars nobody can then find

I tell my smile that it's my only weapon
to make people know what can really happen
and to tell them what is a smile's cost
when it's all you have but you feel lost.

7. STAY

I want you by my side,
even if our hope for 'us' has died.
i can't be on my own,
knowing that you are out there alone.

We are together, bound by a spell,
that's what they say and tell.
our love has no barrier or limit,
it can only increase from a second to minute.

They say that we are unbreakable,
and that our bond is unshakable.
that i'm the club and you're the spade,
even if you leave , they won't let 'us' fade.

The depths of oceans and skies,
they are where our love lies.
you are where my heart belongs,
it is what my soul always longs.

8. WHAT IF?

What if I lie on my death bed?
will your tears for me be shed?
what if i am no longer alive?
will your feelings for me be able to survive?
Will you sit by my grave?
and for my love will you crave ?
will you come and see me every day ?
even if you've got nothing to say?
If you move on, won't you look back?
won't you feel a piece of you lack ?
when you'll walk alone at nights ?
will you be affected by any lights ?
When you'll look above and far,
will you be able to spot me as a star ?
will you walk alone for miles and miles ?
and think about my face and smiles ?

Will you feel alone and lost?
and come to me ,whatever may be the cost ?
will you still love me and cry ?
even after i've already said my goodbye.

9. DOUBTS

Is it supposed to be this way?
is this where I'm going to end my day?
do we just have to sit by the bay?
and think about the things we should say?

All the words that I got inside,
i wonder if i should open up to you wide.
should I keep you by my side?
so that my inner self doesn't collide.

Are you the right person to show my charm,
can I be sure that you will do me no harm?
It's my mind that's hissing,
that there's something important missing.

Your smile tells me to believe the lies,
and there's something about those eyes,
that tells me to love you , being blind,
and that there's no flaw left to find.

The tears and words, I still behold,
cause I don't know and I'm not told.
should I be a coward or someone bold
till I know your heart is warm or cold?

10. MAYBE

May be you care but maybe you don't ,
i crave to know that but I know that I won't .
what if you say the unexpected,
and the whole of me feels completely neglected .
i know your heart is less warm than cold ,
but that's why falling for you makes me bold.
i wonder, will I be able to handle what you say,
or will I just sit and cry by the bay.
but what if you really care ?
and your feelings for me are strong and rare.
what if we both look at the moon ,
and want to see each other happily bloom.
but for now; let's just think about the worst case,
or may be with me both the ideas can keep pace
i can't help but wonder that,
maybe you care or maybe you don't ,
but it can be both ,there is no reason that it won't.

11. SHE

fBeginning of a new heart beat,
ending of a similar one.
life of a girl taken by cheat ,
this should be done to none.

The world needs the girls that they kill,
or one day people will wake up with a shrill.
knowing that the end is near,
trembling will make pace with the fear.

She has a life to live,
whose rights you're not the one to give.
let her do it on her own,
she knows ,she can do it alone.

Your absence to her won't matter,
her's will make your life shatter.
she has some goals to catch,
and don't dare her dreams ,you snatch.

Come to the realization and stop this crime,
or you will regret but won't be able to turn back the time.

12. WHY SO SOON ?

Why did you have to leave,
when the patchwork of memories was yet to weave.
everything was going really well,
but as you left , I was close enough to hell.
I didn't feel the same anymore,
all my feelings were washed back to the shore.
you didn't know, I was going through a lot ,
as had I lost ,my hearts only clot.
after watching you leave, I couldn't step back,
as soon as you left ,I felt a part of me lack .
goodbye was a hard word to a say,
cause we used to meet each other every day.
don't you think it was a bit too soon?
i always missed you at nights while staring at the moon .
since you left I walked alone from dusk till dawn,
it was all about our fate that was born.

13. YOU ARE ON YOUR OWN

Nobody is going to be with you when you're right,
and then either you die or you fight.
everyone will say that you're not alone,
and that till now together the stars have shone.
but now the time has come for you to glow,
otherwise with the gust of wind, you will blow.
hold on tight to your only hope,
and then you'll know that there is always scope.
pass on all your happiness and smiles,
and you'll have enough for all the remaining miles.
be who you are and be strong,
and you'll reach where you actually belong.
all you have to do is love everyone's hate,
and that alone can entirely change your fate.
to the past you should no longer hold,
do what you want to not what you're told.

14. BE MINE

To the oceans and their tides,
and to all the other existing sides.
I can tell that there's pleasure in loving you
and in watching you too.
you are all that I want,
I won't get you is what my broken pieces haunt.
you're my way out of hell,
at least that's what my heart and soul tell.
I'm not ready to declare you lost,
no, not at all, not at any cost.
cause , you are all that I crave,
I don't care if you're coward or brave.
I want you, no matter what,
I can't tell my feelings to shut.
you being mine is what I desire,
my thoughts are what your actions inspire.
'be mine forever' is what says my heart,
come, hand in hand, lets together make a new start.

FIRE & ICE

Fire & ice mixed together in your eyes. I could feel a perfect blend of rage and calmness. felt like a hurricane on its way, ready to wreak everything. but somewhere in my heart, I knew. knew that you'd save me from the destruction. and love me instead. cause the hurricane was coming through your eyes, the eyes that love me and the eyes that I love.

YANG

15. HALF HEART & AN EMPTY SOUL

I wish I could have you
for all that you are
but maybe you hated me
for all that I was
i don't know if
you're ever going to look back
to see if I'm around
or pause to hold my hand
but I surely do,
i would hold your hand even
even when you don't care
i would look for you
even if you're not there
but you just gave me
the bits and pieces
a half heart and an empty soul
enough to make me smile
enough to turn tables
enough to melt me

and enough to see through
i love those broken parts
cause I have them too
and ours seem to fit together
and fix each other just fine.
cause you make me feel alive
even when i feel dead sometimes.

16. THE BLINKING LIGHTS

The streetlights stared blinking
as I walked by
the lights went out
as my feet danced along
i smiled and cried
as long as these was anything left
but that was too soon, wasn't it?
so I sat there until the next morning
to see the flickering happiness
but the opposite happened
as I could see only tears
with the wind they went
and few until they got tried
didn't want to rest
otherwise they'd give up
and want to sit there
until the next night
till the lights started linking again
and till I cried along my dance.

17. FALLEN TOO FAR

My tears dried up while counting
the broken pieces of my heart
and my fingers started trembling
while I was trying to
put together the tiniest parts
but they were so fragile
that a gust of wind
would blow them apart
every now and then
and I would have to
start all over again
my vision got blur because of the constant tears
and I could no longer see
how far the pieces have fallen
so I started losing them
and the spaces remained open
for anyone else to come and fit in
but the rest of the pieces
broke faster than anyone coming to fill the spaces
and a day come when nothing remained

only the dried tears , a blur vision and trembling hands
cause the pieces were too tiny to join
and too far to pick up.

18. TWO BROKEN HEARTS

There were shades of grey
whenever we got close
it seemed that we were cursed
and meant to repel.
our beating hearts
were searching for an escape
from a not so ordinary maze
when we accidently got too for
we fell apart in pieces
mirrors broke and colours faded
whenever we failed to see
that we weren't meant to be
clouds roared and thunder flashed
to remind us that we were
not destined to be together
our fantasies burned up
in the flames before our eyes
we tried so hard to break though
all the curses and chains
but nothing worked and we separated together.

i couldn't help but question our fates
and that how could they possibly
break two hearts,
which were already broken enough

19. TRUTHFUL LIES

*Some lies are true
and some truths are lies
but what lies beyond is what matters
if it makes a life or destroys one
dwells on it or let it dwell
love it fiercely or hate it calmly
all of it is what matters
the raging fire sacrificed lives
because it was trapped in
a chaos of truths and lies
it is not ours to know of
who speaks what
but just ours to feel
of who deserves us
we are the creation of lies
and the formation of truth
we bear the weight
of many untold truths
and unforgiven lies
we beautifully merge them
and call them the "truthful lies"*

20. UNITED BY THE STARS

You are watching the stars
and so am i
but we are far away
for each other to see
how we're twinkling
together alone
when the sky's dark
and the moon
makes the ends meet
but I wonder why not us?
maybe we're not the ends
but tied with them
like unbreakable bonds.
we're far but together
loving the oceans and shores
embracing the distance so much that
it does not make a difference
how far we're from each other
just that how pretty the stars seem

when we see each other in them
cause watching the stars on you
is it much of a difference?

21. THE FLAMES OF FIRE

I want to kiss the flames
of a newly born fire.
hopefully it won't hurt me
if it knows what are one's own
and that we fall in the same plane
i will tell the fire to not
take down memories or photographs
of the spoilt relations
cause ones the ashes remain
there's nothing left to store
and I can't help but wonder that
why does fire dwell on people?
it won't destroy houses anymore
or burn the last kept letters
i don't understand
why wouldn't it choose
to lose sometimes
and let the wind blow it off?

and why does fire choose
to take down people
whom it actually dwells on?

• 36 •

22. BURNING ROD

I have the urge
to touch a burning rod
knowing the fact that it'll hurt
I want to talk to you so bad
wanting for you to be mine
but you won't understand
cause does the rain
ever need the flowers?
i will try another day
maybe text you and come over
even if you push me away
or shoot numerous bullets
aiming at my heart
and throw stones at me
waiting for me to fall
i will still get up and love you
even if you choose to
give me thorns midst the roses
i'd always want to be yours
and want you to be mine
as long as the flowers need rain
and the stars need the sky.

23. LOVERS TO STRANGERS

I allowed myself a little smile
when I read your text
it was worth the wait and love
and I fell a little deeper
into your thoughts
though they were just words.
they made me love you even more
and fall for you, a lot more deeper
i could nearly see you smiling
and i could feel you hugging me
there were knots in my stomach
along with the butterflies
then suddenly I realized that
they were just meaningless words
and the scenarios that I created
and the smile on my lips
just vanished like nothing happened
and you were never really there
it ached terribly.

cause falling for you or not
you never knew

24. TANGLED OR RESOLVED?

I came to you for all I wanted

and it was just love

i never knew that

you lacked it two

maybe I made a mistake

in choosing the right person

but even if you weren't

how did you make your wrong pieces

fall in the right places

and make chaos

your art and Identification

how did you afford to

showcase it even better

felt like it made you feel alive

i am so mind blown

about how you pretended

that the strokes of art were always pretty

that 'tangled' was the new 'resolved'

i really wanted your love but it's alright

cause not all fishes survive in the water

and not all humans go to heaven
i will still love you for yourself alone
your chaos and scars.
for all that you are and will be.

25. LOVE & DEATH

I wish I stayed away
away from the happiness
for it brought me pain
away from the crowd
cause now I can't stand alone
away from your love
cause now its hate
i wish i was warned
about how getting attached
kills you internally
every minute of every day
about how loving someone
is as good as dying
about how falling for someone
may never allow you to get up
about how forgetting one memory
would remind you of a hundred more
i wish tears were more joyous than hurtful
i wish you wanted yourself to stay
more than wanting me to leave

cause then recollecting one memory
would remind me of a thousand more
and even dying would seem satisfying
cause it would be for you
and it would take me to your heaven
keeping me alive in your
memories and thoughts
and that would be enough to bring me back to life.

26. FATE OR DESTINY?

You made me crave
the illusions and hallucinations
cause you're all i live and love
you're within me
everywhere I exist
there's a part of you
that I carry along
cause if I don't then
there's a part of me missing
loving you is like
kissing the angry flames
or breathing underwater
like feeling alive while dying
like feeling happy while crying
like living all over again
i love you enough
to catch shooting stars
to mend every broken heart
to shed all the negatives
to swap everyone's feelings.
i think just not enough
to make you fall in love with me

or care for me like I do
i wish I had you but maybe
we were the brightest errors of destiny
or the worst refusals of our fates.

27. IT'S ALL GONE

I came across my
favourite photograph of us
that we clicked last summer
i looked so happy while
watching you smile
and you had eyes
brighter than the brightest star
i still don't want to let go
of you or the memories
the summer air leaves with
the flashes of us together
like the twinkling of
stars at midnight
or blinking of streetlights
from dust till dawn
like the best time of my
life is already over
you're somewhere out there
with someone else
making somewhat different
memories and conversation
meanwhile I'm here

trying to figure out
how'd i fall so deep for someone
who could leave so easily
with tears is my eyes
and smiles on their face

28. WITHOUT A GOODBYE

Do the stars
leave the sky before morning
do the waves
come by before it's time?
does the sun leave
before the night?
then why did you leave
without a goodbye?
i still see your face
when I close my eyes
that smile worth
a thousand diamonds
those pretty eyes
telling me things I never knew
i feel like there could have been
so much more to us
you left me slamming doors on myself
now I wonder why'd I let you in?
i'm so disappointed by the way
that things ended that i don't

have the courage to love anyone anymore
maybe I didn't deserve your love
but a good bye at least
even if it was falsely true
or evenly odd.

29. CAN WE DO IT AGAIN?

Under the dark sky
and the bright moon
we talked until we slept
it was blissful
to see you smile like that
like the way I do for you
i'm so happy to know
that you love me more
i wish I could have you forever
but you started fading away
like the colours of our memories
you stopped making it happen
when that was all I wanted
you stopped giving me your love
when that's what I was craving for
today, under the dark sky
and the bright moon
i'm writing this cause I miss you
or maybe just the memories
but you exist in them

i see you in everyone
i feel you around me
I want you to come back
and hold me like you used to
again under the dark sky
and the bright moon.

30. A DEFINITE MAYBE?

Do you fantasize me
when you're alone
or when you don't see me
in a crowd
would you call me first
if it were between me
and the moon
and control waves
if I had to cross an ocean
to meet you
or maybe crush thorns
to give me a rose
would you stop being
so pretentions about
not being hurt
when your eyes speak
the truth so well
while hiding it alongside
would you pull back
if you thought that

our love was like cold fire
could you share with me
stories of your sweet sorrow
stay when I leave?
love me when I'm weak?
embrace me when I'm flawed?
would you show me the real illusions?
would you give me a definite maybe?

31. FALL FOR ANOTHER

She could no longer
hide her tears
from the people she cared for
she'd drifted from
her own world
to help someone
mend theirs
she tried so hard to go on
without a breakdown
but it wasn't that easy
or was it?
she had her deepest feelings
dumped from her heart
to her mind
which were too heavy to be
carried by anybody at all
the illusions were tempting
and were too easy to believe in
so she loved people who loved her
left people who left her

and anyway why would
a broken heart refuse to mend itself
the moon stop shining?
on the rose stop blooming?
and how could a heart possibly
survive without falling for another

32. TOO MUCH OR TOO LESS?

I am so terribly broken
that I can't even feel sad anymore
i feel so empty and hollow
that everything affects me
in a way that it doesn't
i'm so tired of being pretentious
that being real feels the same
creating illusions seems hard
cause reality crushes me worse
all my right pieces
seem to fall in the wrong place
when its love that I want
but its hate that I get
when I ask them to stay
but they ask me to leave
it starts hurting more
when I start crying less
so I cry oceans when
they only need rivers
i change the currents

when they just need the tides
i make the stars twinkle
when they want the moon to shine
i can't explain in a way that I can
but i think so much like i don't
and it hurts so much that it shouldn't.

33. BROKEN & SHATTERED

Why is it so hard
to mend someone who's broken?
people are so shattered inside
that it's so hard to make out
who's broken more
their hearts or their souls?
those cracked smiles that
they give like they're
just some random pieces
of puzzled puzzles
who feel helpless and
knowingly , worthless.
who're so clueless
about the thunderstorms
that are covering the clear sky
they're so deeply hollow
that filling them
with anything at all
makes the gap even deeper
they've got no hopes of life from death

RUBEENA KAUR

just from life for death
I don't understand if they're
surviving to feel alive
or just breathing to survive?

34. EMPTY BUT IN LOVE

I waited and waited
for you to come along
and that make things work
i sat still, wondering
if something was wrong with me
you did not care
even then , I loved you
i was empty inside
but ironically
still feeling broken
i cried oceans for you
you returned a drop of it
i loved you with everything
and every part of me
but you loved me partially
maybe with the leftovers pieces
you broke me into memories
a chaos of beautiful patchworks
you left my soul hopeless
and my heart homeless

i mistook you as mine
and my soul as yours
you kept it hostage
and then tossed it outside
with poison mixed inside
it infected my heart
a heart that was once yours too.

35. JUST ONE LAST TIME

I want to hold your hands
just one more time and
interlock my fingers in yours
i want to feel safe with you
and go for walks by the sea
to write journals with you
and watch the stars again
i want to laugh together and
cry too; like we did before
knowing it'll never happen again
i wish I knew about the end
before we ended , so that
i could do everything with you
just one more time when
we could still do it together
cause i know that months later
you'd just be reliving everything
with someone else and better
and I'd still be here
wondering if we could

still be together somehow
and meet again sometime
and if you'd still hold me
if in a hundred lifetimes
you got a chance to?

36. THE TWO DIAMONDS

Look into those eyes of mine
and you'll never want to look away
you'll want to be trapped inside
fall for me and search for chaos
and when I give in to you
you'll know everything I've been through
and that I have a world within
a world of no one else but me
where I'm the pawn and the queen both
where I play alone and win alone
where I rule and be ruled on
you'll know how hard I can love
or the urge to know how it feels to be loved
everything you'll ever want
a spark of hope or a little love
a lot of hurt and pain too.
just look into them
and feel them with all your heart